THE UNLIKELY FRIENDSHIP OF RIVER HUGS AND SUNFLOWER

STORY BY:
APRIL SUNFLOWER

Illustrations by Noelle McDougall

Copyright © 2024 April Sunflower
All rights reserved.
ISBN: 979-8-89324-133-4

No part of this publication shall be reproduced, transmitted, or sold in whole or in part in any form without prior written consent of the author, except as provided by the United States of America copyright law. Any unauthorized usage of the text without express written permission of the publisher is a violation of the author's copyright and is illegal and punishable by law. All trademarks and registered trademarks appearing in this guide are the property of the author.

DEDICATION

This book is dedicated to all of the young people who are currently living in the shadow of society's myths of what it means to be normal, worthy, and whole. May you know your own worth, embrace your gifts, share your truth, and discover your path to a joyous life journey.

TABLE OF CONTENT

CHAPTER ONE..2
   Sunflower and Fern Find the Big Dipper

CHAPTER TWO..4
   Sunflower Meets River Hugs

CHAPTER THREE...5
   My Beans, My Choice!

CHAPTER FOUR...8
   Later That Day

CHAPTER FIVE...10
   Carrots and Love

CHAPTER SIX..11
   "Oh, That Bear, Again!"

CHAPTER SEVEN..14
   Mr. Hugs' and Sunflower's Hearts

CHAPTER EIGHT..16
   Love and the Universe

Chapter One

Sunflower and Fern Find the Big Dipper

Sunflower is a small white rabbit who hops and talks differently than other rabbits. She lives in Strawberry Moon. Thankfully, she has a best friend in Strawberry Moon. Their name is Fern.

Fern is a large horse. Sunflower's mom was best friends with Fern's mom and dad. Sunflower's mom was named Lilac Grace, and Fern's parents were Bay and Clover.

When Sunflower was a little bunny, she couldn't hop very far. So Fern got down on the ground and told her to climb up on their back. She pulled their fur, and it hurt. But Fern didn't mind that much.

Over time, Fern stopped thinking about their fur being pulled by Sunflower.
And they rode together from sun up to sun down all over Strawberry Moon. They even rode in the rain and the snow.

As Sunflower and Fern grew, they rode further and farther from Strawberry Moon. One day, they rode all the way to the end of the Star Trail and ended up in the Big Dipper.

Sunflower and Fern weren't scared of a big city like the Big Dipper. They both like adventure. Plus, Fern knew the way back to Strawberry Moon. Just follow the Star Trail till you reach the other end. As soon as the sun starts going down, the Star Trail is easy to find.

Chapter Two

SUNFLOWER MEETS RIVER HUGS

Sunflower and Fern both find the Big Dipper exciting and busy. She especially loves seeing shows on stage in the Big Dipper. Fern likes wandering around and sticking their nose inside every open window and door.

In the Big Dipper, there are rows and rows of new and exciting shows for Sunflower. And in the middle of all the theaters sits a circle with a ticket booth.

Over the years, she became a well-known visitor to that booth, the one with the bright purple roof.

One day, she was waiting in line when a bear noticed she had what humans call a "disability." But her mother, Lilac Grace, taught her to think differently about how she hops and talks.

Lilac Grace said, "Nature makes every living creature unique, and you are my lovely bunny, Sunflower, who is just unique."

The bear said, "Hi, I am River Hugs" to Sunflower. He also said, "I manage this ticket booth with the bright purple roof."

Of course, Sunflower knows most creatures care a lot about the way she hops and talks. So sometimes, they don't take the time to get to know her and learn about her many gifts.

Sunflower still felt a little thankful when Mr. River Hugs kindly asked, "May I help you pick out a show?" So she happily handed him her list of shows.

Chapter Three

My Beans, My Choice!

Sunflower was proud of her list of shows. She read about each show and wrote down her top ten picks.

She also color-coded her list by type of show and noted how far she had to hop to each show.

When she gave River Hugs her list, she thought he would agree that it was a very fine list. To her surprise, he nodded his head from side to side and said, "No, these shows are not right for you…none of these will do."

He told Sunflower about the shows for families with little bunnies. He believed such shows were better for a bunny like her. But she knew that Mr. Hugs saw her "disability" and thought she was a little, helpless bunny that he needed to protect.

The more he tried to talk her into a different show— the more she got upset and wanted to get away from him as quickly as any bunny hops. Eventually, he gave up trying to change her mind and said, "They are your beans—I suppose." Finally, she gave him some beans, then hopped away with a ticket to one of her shows.

Mr. Hugs didn't know that Sunflower earned her beans all on her own. Actually, he didn't really know her at all. And she, well, she also didn't know him.

Chapter Four

Later That Day

Next, Sunflower found a place to grab a veggie burger and get some water. As she sat in the warm sun enjoying her lunch, she realized — if she was a human cartoon character, steam would still be coming out of her ears.

So she told herself "to just breathe…no sense in letting a perfectly lovely day turn into a bad day." Her mother taught her well.

Lilac Grace always said, "Look up towards the sky, hold your ears high, then just go about your bunny business." She took in and let out three more deep breaths. Then, she did exactly what her mother taught her to do.

She said to herself if I see that Mr. River Hugs again, then I am going to say — "Excuse me, Mr. Hugs, but I am a grown rabbit and not a helpless bunny!"

Later that afternoon, Sunflower really enjoyed her show. Then she safely rode on Fern's back home to Strawberry Moon.

Chapter Five

CARROTS AND LOVE

Fern often asks Sunflower, "What makes your carrots grow so sweet?" And she always looks up at the sky.

And with her lopsided smile and that voice of hers so unique, she says:
"Love...love makes almost everything and everyone sweet in this world...love is everywhere if you believe with your heart that love is always in the universe."

Truthfully, Fern doesn't know if what Sunflower believes about love and carrots is so. They figure carrots grow from sun, soil, and water. But then again, who really knows? There is a lot for creatures to consider, and love seems confusing to all creatures.

Sunflower's mom, Lilac Grace, taught Sunflower how to grow her own carrots. She didn't want Sunflower to be hungry. Fern agrees that part is love.

Fern supposes that is how love grows. And if love grows ponies, bunnies, and friends, why not carrots too?

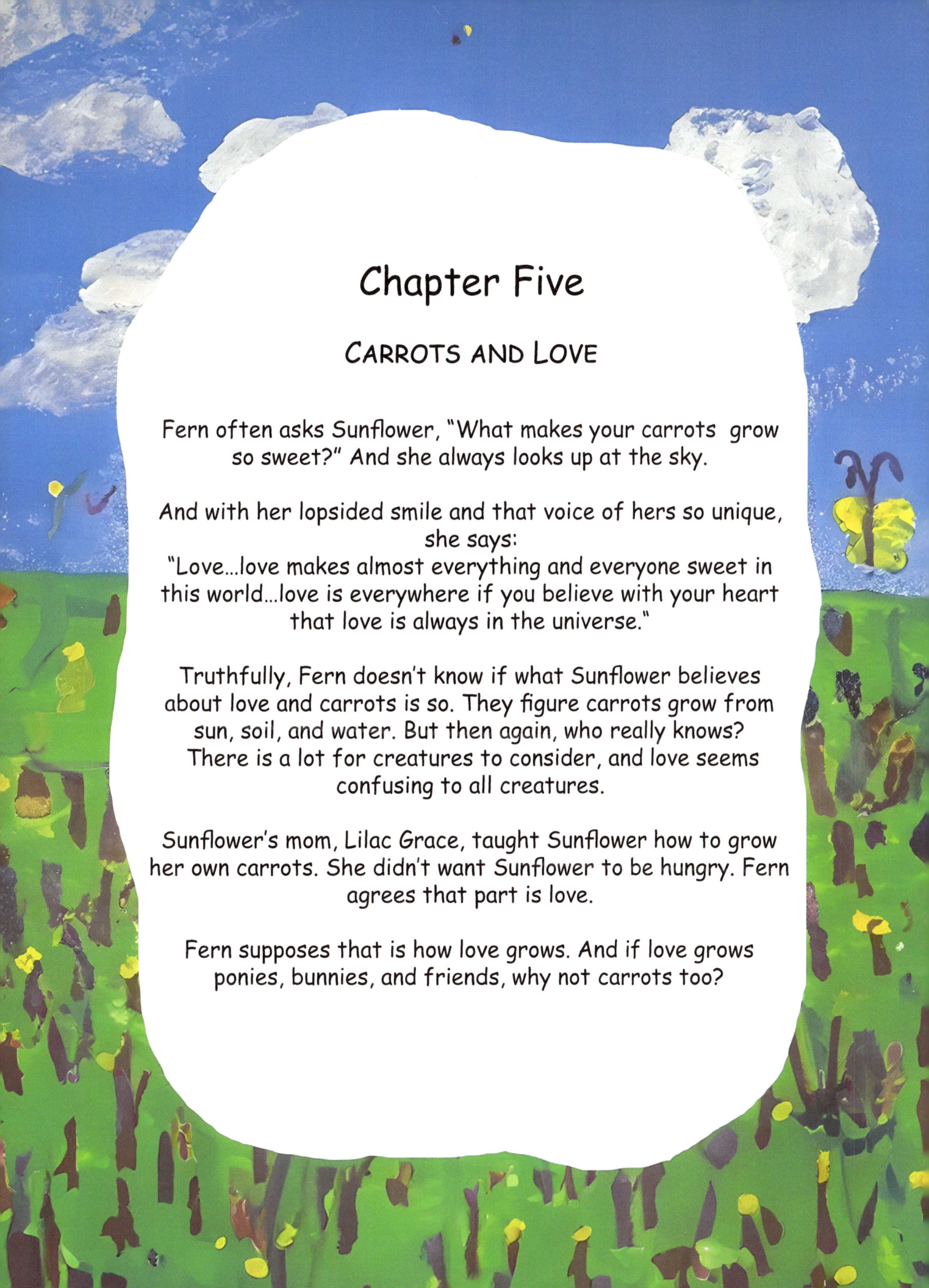

Chapter Six

"Oh, That Bear, Again!"

A few months passed by, and Sunflower had enough beans for another show. So, on Fern's back, she rode to the Big Dipper. Then she hopped to that booth, the one with the bright purple roof.

And wouldn't you know — River Hugs spotted her in line again and started towards her with a big smile. She rolled her eyes and said to herself, "NOT this bear, again — please, oh, please, can't another creature help me?"

Sunflower was pleasantly surprised when Mr. Hugs said, "Nice to see you again," and then helped her get a ticket to her first choice of shows. This time, he didn't say much to her at all. But most important to her, he didn't try once to change her mind.

As time went on and the two of them crossed paths every few months outside that booth — yes, the one with the bright purple roof — Mr. Hugs started rushing to greet her.

Mr. Hugs enjoyed talking about shows with Sunflower and looked forward to seeing her. She liked calling him Mr. Hugs. Sometimes, she looked forward to his hugs, most of all.

Sunflower and Mr. Hugs became good theater buddies. And from time to time, she wondered what happened to change his heart. Did another creature say something to him? Did he take a class?

Chapter Seven

Mr. Hugs' and Sunflower's Hearts

Then, one day, Sunflower was sitting in the booth — correct, the one with the bright purple roof — chatting with Mr. Hugs like old theater buddies do — when he looked at her and said," You know I talk about you...I hope you don't mind."

By now, he knew her well enough to understand that look on her face. She was thinking it all depends on what you say about me if I mind!

Mr. Hugs responded to her look with, "I tell them all, when you make up your mind, a bulldozer couldn't stop you...because you are a strong and smart rabbit."

The more he talked from his heart—the clearer how he changed became to her. She realized changing for him wasn't nearly as hard as she made it out to be. He simply noticed what upset her, then told himself not to make the same mistake twice.

Once he decided to do better, he saw much more than her "disability" and found reasons to get to know her. Could changing really be that simple and quick? It surely appears to be so for Mr. Hugs.

Then Sunflower made what she thought was a horrible mistake of her own by saying what was in her own heart. As soon as the words tumbled from her mouth, she felt so ashamed of herself.

She wished for a rabbit hole to open up and swallow her whole and for Mr. Hugs to never see her again. She accidentally said, "I love you." When no rabbit hole appeared, she looked up at his face, and with a huge grin, he said, "You are in my heart...so of course, I love you, too."

Mr. Hugs taught Sunflower that changing your heart can be as simple as paying attention to other's feelings and trying to do a little better. And then, just maybe, you might discover someone who you can enjoy and learn to love.

Chapter Eight

LOVE AND THE UNIVERSE

In the end, River Hugs proved Sunflower's theory that love is always in the universe for her to find. All she needs to do is believe and search with an open heart.

Sunflower believes:
Love is in the warmth of sunshine.
Love is on the moon and in the night sky. Love swirls all around her in the wind.
Love is in the music that makes her rabbit ears dance. Love is in the paintings that make her face smile.

Love is in the shows and books that make her want to cry.
Love floats down on snowflakes that tickle her nose. Love skips across the river behind her rabbit hole.
Love sinks into the ground when Fern runs.
Love always drips from rainbows and coats planet Earth.

And how about you? Do you believe too?

Love is certainly in the raindrops that grow Sunflower's carrots, which are so sweet.
Love may even be in the weeds that itch her paws. Love was definitely on Lilac Grace's mind when she taught Sunflower to grow carrots.
Love is for sure in Fern's heart when they carry her on their back.
Love sometimes just slips from her mouth.

Now, we all know that love stirs in River Hugs' soul when he changes his heart.

And love can still surprise unique Sunflowers — even creatures who know when you believe love is always in the universe, you are never all alone.

THANK YOU NOTES

HUGS TO YOU ALL!

First, thank you to Joy, Kathy, and Beth, who responded to my writing this book with "I love that idea for you." Here's to many more years of friendship!

Next, thank you to Matt, who connected me to Noelle. You are one of the good guys!

Of course, a special thanks to Noelle. Thank you for sharing your gifts with us all. Thank you for your patience while I figured out my process. I am sure this is the first of many books for you.

Thank you to the many folks who listened to my internal debates over my character development and vision of inclusion. While it feels like too many of you to mention here by name, please know that you are forever in my heart. I am grateful for each of your time and talents.

A special final shoutout to Daryl, whose actions and deeds inspired Mr. River Hugs to turn over and over in my mind. May the universe always return to you all of the kindness and love that you give to others. And may I always be fortunate enough to know someone like you.

ABOUT THIS BOOK

Join best friends, Sunflower and Fern, on their adventure from Strawberry Moon to the Big Dipper. Will Sunflower, who hops and talks differently than other rabbits, make a new friend? Or will Sunflower's pride get in the way of her making friends with River Hugs?

Children and adults alike will enjoy getting to know Sunflower and reading about her love growing friendships. This witty, poetic story, is cheerfully complimented by the book's colorful hand-painted illustrations.

In addition to enjoying this book, children may wish to experiment with drawing and painting their favorite characters from the book. Grown-ups will also appreciate the life lessons from Sunflower's mother, Lilac Grace, who insisted that Sunflower knew how to take care of herself.

This book is a long time dream of the author who has a lifelong disability herself and grew-up wishing for positive characters with disabilities in children's books. After her introduction to a talented young artist, the author's dream of one day publishing an inclusive children's book became reality.

BY: APRIL SUNFLOWER

AUTHOR PROFILE

April Sunflower identifies first as a person with a lifelong disability who speaks with a CP accent. She holds a BA in Sociology and has always been interested in the portrayal of people with disabilities in literature. Writing a children's book with a strong, independent disabled female character was a lifelong dream of hers.

April Sunflower began her professional career providing peer counseling services for a small non-profit. Later, she worked on disability policy issues, training, and system change projects. Eventually, she was recruited into the Federal government, and she is now retired after more than twenty-two years of Federal service.

In her private life, April Sunflower continues to be a passionate advocate at the intersection of disability with race, gender, and religion. In addition to writing and reading, she also really enjoys painting, the theater, ice cream, and doggy kisses.

MEET THE ILLUSTRATOR

Noelle McDougall is so excited to be a part of this project about inclusion and acceptance. Diagnosed with Prader-Willi syndrome as a young child, she has worked hard to face all of the challenges that have come her way. Currently, Noelle loves riding horses, crafting, volunteering, hanging with her family, and painting. Noelle shares that she never would have had the opportunity to create the illustrations for this book without her connections with Indicator Art (which offers virtual classes for individuals with disabilities). Noelle would like to thank her parents for their love and support, Matt Palmo (of Indicator Art) for all of his encouragement and guidance, and especially April for this awesome opportunity!